When Someone You Love Completes Suicide

THIS IS SURVIVABLE!

By Sondra Sexton-Jones, M.S., L.P.C., L.M.F.T.

©Copyright 1996
Centering Corporation
All rights reserved.
Revised 2020

ISBN-10: 1561231673
ISBN-13: 978-156123167-6

Centering is a non-profit,
bereavement resource center.

CENTERING CORPORATION
—— AND ——
GRIEF DIGEST MAGAZINE
GRIEF RESOURCES

www.centering.org

Phone: 866-218-0101

In Loving Memory of:

Name: _____

Born: _____

Died: _____

That which we lose we mourn,
but we must rejoice that we ever had.
C.J. Wells

For my future:

Hailey Nichole Lester

Lexie Kristen Sexton

Callie Mae Sexton

Christopher Cody Sexton

A Note from the Author

Surviving a death is to endure dreadful pain. Surviving a death by suicide is to descend into Hell. It is often coupled with the added burden of public embarrassment, private shame and humiliation. If those were not enough to contend with, waves of anger and guilt may consume every waking moment for a long time. You will be profoundly changed by the event.

The fact that you are reading this suggests you have not only decided to survive, but to live, and to live to the best of your ability.

You can survive. ***This is survivable!***

My Story

Four months past his 52nd birthday, my husband, Ray, pulled his truck into our garage and stretched a piece of garden hose from the tail-pipe to the cab. In a very short time, he was dead of carbon monoxide poisoning.

We had been married five years, seven months, eight days.

It was nearly 11:00 PM when I returned home from school. As I passed the two big windows on the front of the house, I noticed that no lights were on inside. Odd, I thought.

I opened the front door and an appalling, unrecognizable odor snaked into my nostrils, burning deep into my lungs. My eyes teared. Instinctively, I reached for the light switch. The light thinly penetrated the blackness. I gasped for air; what I sucked in clawed at my throat and lungs and they revolted. I slapped a hand over my mouth to suppress the bile crawling up the back of my throat. Moving through the house, fear and panic grew with each step.

Rushing to the den, I flipped on the light. No Ray. No note. No sign of my cat or poodle. No sound but a strange clicking and the wild barking of Ray's dogs. Fear and choking panic grew with each step I took. My heart thudded heavily and loudly in my ears. I moved to our bedroom, pushing the door open with such force that it bounded halfway shut again. I flipped on the light. The bed was empty, unmade, covers thrown back in Ray's customary manner that made an almost perfect triangle across the bed. Summer, my poodle and Pug, my cat, dashed from the odorous confines of the stinking room.

I made my way the short distance out of the room, through the kitchen to the garage. The clicking, now very loud, reverberated through the hot house. Between me and a world upside down was a solitary ash paneled door.

I grabbed for the doorknob, quickly jerking my hand away from its heat. Reaching again, I yanked the door open. Excruciating heat rolled over me and pungent odor exploded in my face. I reached for the light switch. The brightness of three 100-watt bulbs slashed jaggedly through the blackness. Ray's two dogs were lunging and biting at the truck tires, frothing at their mouths. I saw what I thought was a shoulder in the cab of the truck. I heard a voice scream Ray's name as I ran to the driver's side and jerked open the door.

What was before me was not registering. I saw and did not believe. I saw and did not see. Jerking the keys from the ignition, I raced outside, the dogs following me, gasping for fresh air. I needed help. I needed someone to take care of Ray. He was bleeding. No, not bleeding. Oh no, this couldn't be happening!

The lights from my neighbor's den cast a soft serene glow through their back door. I pounded hard on the glass door, screaming their names. Strangers move wordlessly through a house after a suicide. Close neighbors arrived, then watched silently as police and paramedics went about their jobs. I tried to grasp what was happening. I felt as if I had been dropped into molasses. Soft-spoken strangers asked questions I could not answer. "I don't know," rolled out of my mouth like a priest's litany. I sat, swaddled in an invisible blanket of numbness, separating me from those in the room. A few short hours ago, Ray and I had felt each other's breath. Now he was dead – and by his own hand.

That part of me that had always operated well in crisis situations insisted on pushing me toward what I should be doing. I realized I was holding my address book. Then I remembered – telephone calls.

Moving my finger methodically down the page and through each name, I finally found the ones I needed. When I was able to tell them what had happened, they told me they would be at the house as quickly as possible.

Until that night, my life was neat, normal, everything in place. I was a graduate student at Texas Woman's University, finishing my master's degree in marriage and family therapy.

Ray's career had been impacted by downtimes in the oil industry. He left the small company he was with and talked about starting a business. It had been frustrating. But this?

Why was never far from my thoughts. I became a woman possessed. I wanted answers. I quizzed friends, people he had worked with, family. No one had answers. His friends of twenty years reinforced Ray's persona of always appearing able to handle everything.

I was awash with guilt. I was a professional. What had I missed? I was his wife. I should have known! I failed my husband – my family – my profession.

Why would not stop rolling around inside. I looked through his billfold. When I found a business card with M.D. after the name, I was both stunned and elated. He was ill and had not told me. But the card was nothing more than a business contact.

Weeks passed before I could bring myself to call the medical examiner. There had been no autopsy since the cause of death was clear. I did not know then, nor now, if Ray had reason to question his health.

It was all I could do to manage the paralyzing pain that swept over me.

At times, I was unable to manage at all.

This time was also filled with trigger events that drew me back to that horrific night:

I had great difficulty re-entering the garage and refused to drive my car into it until winter's wrath made it mandatory.

Exhaust fumes made me gag. The first time the effect was so powerful, I walked into the house, straight to the kitchen sink and vomited. Fear of being trapped inside a dark house was terrifying, so I kept lights on throughout my home.

The 23rd of the month was a difficult day for a long time, particularly when it fell on a Wednesday.

Then there were the crazies – my attempt to deal with unbridled pain. The first occurred the morning after Ray's death. Standing at the door of our bedroom, I stared at the bedcovers as he had left them. The sheets, with their soft pink flowers seemed objectionable in the new circumstances. With quiet fury, I pulled them from the bed and methodically shredded the king-sized sheets into spaghetti like strings. I still have no recollection as to what I did with the pile of material.

I would stand in his closet, wrapping his clothes about me, drinking in his smell. His platform rocker sat in mute testimony to one gone. I alternated between sitting in it, curling up like an infant, and flailing at it – screaming at his absence. Finally, I removed the chair. But for a while, since the object of my anger was out of reach, it was great to have somewhere to direct the rage.

I searched out those special places where we had spent time. In the quiet of the house, I pulled out keepsakes of cards, notes, and sketches that had passed between us and I touched the richness of shared expressions of love.

I felt an incredible pull to his grave. At first it was to see the scarred earth, to reinforce the reality of his death. I talked to him, screamed at him. I leaned against the headstone. Sometimes, in my desperate need to experience his nearness, I would lay down, my body stretched lengthwise over his grave.

My energy level was incredibly high despite sleeping and eating very little. Nights were the worst. Weeks passed before I could make myself get back into our bed. I could not dislodge the memory of him sleeping peacefully that fateful morning and how betrayed I felt. I painted the inside of the house four times in eight months. I talked and repeated stories and thoughts and perceptions of Ray incessantly to our friends, Fred and Lucy. In their kindness, they listened each time as intensely as if it were the first.

It takes a long time to digest death, and in trying to do so, we are transmuted into new people, never again to be what we were, innocent from some of the horrors life throws our way. The pieces of my life's puzzle will never again fit together as they once did.

It never occurred to me not to be open and honest about Ray's death. I did not want it veiled, though I was cautioned by well-meaning colleagues that perhaps I, myself, was causing professional suicide. But the overriding need to be able to come to terms with what had happened, ruled. What's more, if I expected my clients to operate openly and honestly, I could do no less.

We process life's events in ways most comfortable to us. Some of us talk. Some read. Some journal. Some stuff everything in a big emotional box and shove it into a dark hole only to have it resurface at the most unexpected times and circumstances. I process by talking, reading, and journaling, but mostly talking. For a survivor, talking is imperative. Talking makes the event real, lessens the power of what happened, and ultimately diffuses the horror so that it becomes more manageable.

There came a time when I decided I would live. Having decided that, I didn't have a clue as to how to go about it, so I muddled through a few months trying to keep up with schoolwork. What I recognized one day was that I wanted to do more than just survive my husband's suicide. I wanted substance and meaning in my life.

That meaning surfaced one stormy night at my clinic when a panicked client brought her friend in for help. The young woman had been discovered sitting on the edge of her bed with the muzzle of a 38 stuck in her mouth. She wanted a release from her pain and had decided that ending her life would take care of everything. She had an eight-year-old daughter and was convinced the daughter would be better off and would soon forget how her mother died.

For the first time, I understood the saying: You can never really know someone until you walk a mile in their shoes. The irony is, shoes or not, we still will not know that person.

> *Reality is, we can only second guess what that person is feeling.*
> *Reality is, we do not have control over someone else's behavior.*
> *Reality is, we do not have the power to make anyone want to live.*
> *Reality is, we cannot live for them.*

And in that moment, I understood as never before that I was not responsible for my husband's completing suicide. I know I am not responsible for any other person's choice to take their own lives. I looked at the young woman before me, filled with such despair. "I cannot live for you." I told her. "I cannot make you want to live. I cannot breathe for you. I cannot make you want to breathe." She was as still as a stone. "But I am here. I am willing to walk with you. I am willing to help you explore possibilities and options."

In the book, **Dante's Inferno**, Dante spoke of going through the dark wood. I have moved through and away from the dark wood in increments. With each successful cycle of significant dates came a strength, a quiet awareness of a growing calmness resting deep inside my being.

When I heard Edwin Shneidman, founder of the American Association of Suicidology speak, I grappled and fought against his saying that suicide is consistent with the rest of the person's life. Those who complete suicide typically don't cope well with difficulties and appear to have limited capacities for psychological pain. They have a penchant for constricted, either/or, black/white thinking, and a history of running from problems.

But in the cold light of day, removed from the emotion of the moment, the description fit Ray like a glove. He persisted with things long past the point of needing to be relinquished, and his refusal to follow advice or to accept help was legendary among our friends. I will never have answers to all the questions about his choice to complete suicide. Answers are as far from my reach as he is. I know that his was not the act of one crazed. It was instead the act of a man crumpled, thwarted by life, who not only didn't fight back, but would not, could not talk about what troubled him.

In my typical hurry-up fashion, I expected the agony of that night to be over and done with rather quickly. Fact is, it will never be over and done with. It will always be a part of who I am and how I look at life. Certainly, the pain has diminished into sadness. Ray thought there was no other way for him. I no longer grieve the future that he took away from us. And, thankfully, the triggering events rarely occur. When they do, they are manageable now.

Changes in my life have been enormous. There is little I take for granted. I am much more aware of the fragility of life. Suffice to say I know far more about loss, reconciliation and living than do many. I know about giving up responsibility for another's life.

I have learned that each of us is responsible for our own lives, for living them – or ending them. And I know about surviving.

Someone once told me that Ray's life must not be judged by the event that took him from us. In this life, he was a caring, nurturing, compassionate human being. His manner of leaving cannot diminish that fact.

Because of Ray's death, suicide has a permanent place in my vocabulary and in my life. Suicide has a permanent place in my soul, and I am both stronger and more vulnerable – and more compassionate – because of it.

What was before me was not registering. I saw and did not believe. I saw and did not see. Jerking the keys from the ignition, I raced outside, the dogs following me, gasping for fresh air. I needed help. I needed someone to take care of Ray. He was bleeding. No, not bleeding. Oh no, this couldn't be happening!

Impact

Whether you found the body or you were told what happened, the moment petrifies in your mind. Never in a nightmare could anything have been more hellish or prepared me for what I saw: Ray, body swollen, left side of his face crimson, skin stretched tight, split jaggedly at the edge of his mouth, his eye and his ear. The right side of his face molded its swollenness against the car seat. Dark mucus puddled around his mouth and nose. His right arm was stretched out, his long fingers curled gently toward his palm. He had lain himself down and waited to die.

Triggering events – powerful recurrent emotional surges, become grounded into your experience. Things usually benign take on sinister qualities. For example, if you received the news by telephone while at work, the first time the phone rings after returning to work may wipe you out.

It was clear to me why I vomited when I smelled exhaust fumes. Some reactions may seem to be without rhyme or reason. Usually, however, you understand why you react the way you do and that can allow you to take care of yourself in a more nurturing way.

You need to know:

Living or dying by suicide is a choice.
    That choice rests solely with the individual.
    Their death is not about you.
You are not responsible for your loved one's death.
    You will never really understand why they chose to die.

Your physical well-being will be in a constant state of flux.

You may feel good one moment, horrible the next.

It is normal to experience great bursts of physical energy, to need little or no rest.

Your body is absorbing a great emotional hurt.

You will come to a moderate place again.

It is also normal to have a period when you need extra sleep.

Your body is conserving energy for healing.

Your energy will return.

Respect your physical needs, and honor your body.

You can expect:

To have bouts of annoying illnesses, gastric problems such as upset stomachs, more colds and allergies.

Your body is under great stress, too.

Your eyes may not focus properly.

You may be uncoordinated.

This will pass; you will return to your former level of health.

An increase in physical pain.

You may believe you need to suffer.

Take care of yourself by eating well.

Get a physical.

To experience the sensation that you are unable to breathe.

You can breathe.

Take slow, deep breaths.

As you begin to heal, these symptoms will decrease.

Your creative energy will be less than magnificent.

Your memory is not lost.

You will regain the ability to retain information.

The creative forces will return.

You may:

Have nightmares.

Be unable to concentrate.

Feel an acute sense of embarrassment and humiliation.
> This is not about you. This is about your loved one.

Be deeply disillusioned with life.

Experience either an increase or a decrease in your appetite.

Believe you have seen your loved one.

Be unable to recall the face of your loved one.

Believe you hear your loved one encouraging you to join him in death.
> This is a wish to be with your loved one.
> You do not have to act on these thoughts. You can survive.

What helps:

Pamper yourself now and then.
> Get a massage, and if you feel like crying, do so.
> Take a bubble bath.
> Put fresh flowers in your room.
> See a favorite movie.
> Take a walk someplace beautiful.
> Go to a park and swing.
> Drink hot tea from a special cup.

Eat healthy food.
> Cut up fruits and veggies to eat, even if you're not hungry.
> Treat yourself to a comfort food now and then, like cookies.
> Drink a lot of water.

Stay away from alcohol and drugs – they can prolong grief.
Buy and take a multivitamin.

Make your body move.
>Walk, run or jog.
>Play basketball, softball, volleyball: something physical.
>Even if you don't feel like moving, move.

Work from lists.
>Lists help decrease frustration with a poor memory.
>Make small "possible accomplishments" lists.
>A list will help organize your day.
>A list provides structure.
>You are not inadequate, just hurting.

Grief is a multi-layered experience, threading its way through your physical self and your emotional self. You are learning to live without your loved one, day by day, and sometimes, moment by moment. You will be profoundly changed by this event.

You have been gravely wounded.
Your body needs to heal.
This is survivable.

It never occurred to me not to be open and honest about Ray's death. I did not want it veiled, though I was cautioned by well-meaning colleagues that perhaps I was causing professional suicide. But the overriding need to be able to come to terms with what had happened, ruled. What's more, if I expected my clients to operate openly and honestly, I could do no less.

Facing the Sad Reality

No matter where you turn, there is no escaping the fact your loved one chose to die. This kind of death can make you feel abandoned and rejected. Your self-esteem is smashed. Emotions are greatly exaggerated. You may feel worthless and think of yourself as a failure. Feelings of guilt, that you could have or should have done more, surface. Some people believe they are somehow responsible for their loved one's death.

Living or dying is a choice.
That choice rests solely with the individual.
Their death is not about you.

For some, death by suicide is just too much to face. They refuse to accept the sad reality of the suicide. The death is explained away as an accident. Others work their way through the grief and move on. Many times, facing the death brings searching, searching for information that will help answer the why.

Why *was never far from my thoughts. I became a woman possessed – I wanted answers. I quizzed friends, people he had worked with, family. No one had answers. His friends of twenty-five years reinforced Ray's persona of appearing to be able to handle everything.*

Remember, no one grieves exactly as you do. Your experience cannot be seen or felt through the eyes of anyone else. The intensity and duration are uniquely your own.

There is no right or wrong way to grieve. There is just your way.

You need to know:

Your religious and spiritual beliefs may be challenged.

You may fantasize that your loved one died because of foul play.
      Suicide is hard to believe.

It is normal to question whether or not you want to live.
      This comes on the wings of fear of the unknown.
      You will grow more secure in your will to live.

You will never know everything about your loved one.
      You only know what your loved one allowed you to know.
      We all have secret rooms known only to ourselves.

Grief is a process.
The pain will not last forever.
You will grow beyond the event.

You can expect:

To feel the need for a more fixed routine.
      This helps you create a feeling of safety.
      It provides order in your life after chaos.

To feel an intense identification with your loved one, even to thinking that your death by suicide is inevitable.
      It is not. You can choose to live.

To want details about the last few moments of their life:
      Did they suffer?
      Did they think of me, of us?
            Ask! These questions make the event real.
            You are searching to see how you fit into their life,
            to determine your importance to them.
A need to talk about your loved one.
      This is normal.

This is one way of keeping your loved one close.
You will slowly digest the death and the details.

To focus on your loved one's suffering.
Be gentle with yourself. You are very raw with pain.
You are not responsible for their choice.
You can survive.

Remember, living or dying is a choice. That choice rests solely with the individual. Their death is not about you.

You can expect:

To feel a need to make sweeping changes.
Move slowly.
Thinking clearly is difficult.

To initially idealize your loved one.
You are likely to push away what was at times annoying.
You may forget what was frustrating about them.
Eventually, you will be able to recall and appreciate the person for who they were, flaws and all.

To be unable to recall readily what your loved one looked like or to remember the sound of her voice.
These abilities will return.
They are not lost forever.

To grieve for the lost future with your loved one.

Your journey through grief is unique to you.
Be gentle with yourself.
You are very raw with pain.
You are not responsible for their choice.
You can survive.

You may:

Find you are locked into your own thoughts.
>Being consumed by what has happened is normal.
>It takes time to digest what has happened.

Question who you are and whether or not you will recover.

Not believe your loved one is dead.

Experience the world as a frightening place.
>Your view of the world has changed.
>You will regain your balance.
>Experience ruptures in relationships.
>Some friends and family will push you to "be better and get on with life" before you are ready.
>You will be angry at their lack of sensitivity.
>They are struggling with how to help and what to do for you.
>Give yourself permission to take the time you need to grieve.

Experience the memory of the event in exquisite clarity.

Feel incompetent to deal with everyday tasks.
>You are not incompetent.
>You are struggling with an abnormal circumstance.

Withdraw from the world, as if everything is too difficult.

Walk with your shoulders hunched forward.

Drench yourself in memories.
>Grief is a process. The pain will not last forever.
>You will grow beyond the event.

Be overly vigilant of danger.
>The world as you once knew it has shattered.
>The world now feels like a frightening place.
>This will pass.

It is important to remember you will grieve in your own unique way. You are the only one who has experienced your life and who feels as you do about what has happened. You are the only one who has been through what came into your life. You are the only one who experienced the death of your loved one from your perspective.

I was awash with guilt. I was a professional. What had I missed? I was his wife. I should have known! I failed my husband – my family – my profession.

The Roller Coaster of Emotions

Someone you love has ended their life – an unfathomable act. During this early period, you will attempt to deny and avoid the reality of what has happened. You will experience the icy shock of the event as well as the disbelief this tragedy could invade your world. Your feelings will wax and wane, fold one onto the other and have no pattern. It can feel terrible, and it's normal.

You need to know:

Your emotions may feel dead for a time.
> This numbness is your shock absorber.
> Clutch it closely to you.
> It is saving you from being savaged by overwhelming feelings.

Intense anger and rage are both common.
> It's okay to be angry with them.
> It's okay to be angry at everything.

You may feel as if you're falling apart.
> Understand this is a form of clearing pain so you can heal.
> It is the death of the old from which the new will regenerate.

You may feel as if you're drifting through the days.
> It is not yet real.

You may feel that you cannot live without or be happy without them.
    You lived before, were a whole person before.
    Your life is not defined by them.
    Your life was enriched by their presence.

You may feel overwhelming sadness.
    You don't always have to be strong and bear up.
    Howl with your pain.
    Cry and cry and cry.

You are still a lovable person.
The pain will toughen and yet soften you.

You can expect:

To feel intense anger at the person who chose to die, at friends and family who want you to feel better so they will be more comfortable around you, at doctors, the system, teachers, and all those who touched your loved one. And at yourself, when you think you could have done something.

To have good days and bad days.

To have laughter and unexpected joy.

The images of the death to diminish in their intensity.

To think you are going crazy.

To overreact to the smallest of irritations and frustrations.

Grief is a process.
The pain will not last forever.
You will grow beyond the event.

There will be times when you will reel with emotions so powerful that you may question your ability to survive. Emotions and feelings are survivable, no matter how intense they become. Despite feeling as if you are going crazy, everything you experience during this time is appropriate and normal in this abnormal situation.

Emotions will be exaggerated. You may feel trapped in volatile, large feelings. These will lessen. You will not always be so acutely sensitive.

Fall headlong into your grief, for in doing so fully, you will move through it, clearing a path for the future.

> *Be gentle with yourself, for you are raw with pain.*
> *You are not responsible for their choice.*
> *You can survive.*

To envy those you see being happy with their mates, children, parents, grandparents, friends.
> They are not flaunting what they have.
> They are just living their lives.
> You are very sensitive to what you have lost.

To think of and want sex if you have lost an intimate relationship.
> It is a natural need and want.
> Do not condemn yourself for having those feelings.
> These feelings call you toward life.

You can expect:

Holidays, anniversaries, birthdays and other special days to bring intense feelings of loneliness.
> You may feel at a loss as to what to do.
> Make plans for the occasion well before the special day.

To feel relief the ordeal is over if your loved one had held you hostage to the threat of taking their own life.
> It is normal to be glad the ordeal is over.
> It is normal to believe you could have done more.
> It is normal to resent their choice.
> It is normal to be angry at the control they had over you.
> Remember – they had to decide whether to live or die.

An odd by-product of my loss is that I'm aware of being an embarrassment to everyone I meet. I see people, as they approach me, trying to make up their minds whether they'll say something about it or not. I hate it if they do, and if they don't.

C.S. Lewis, **A Grief Observed**

You may:

Want to take your own life rather than to work through the pain.

> You do not have to end your life because of your devotion.
> You can choose to live, and to live well.

Experience explosive emotional reactions to certain events, circumstances or situations that cause you to revisit the moments when you learned of your loved one's death.

> These are sometimes called triggering events.
> These are normal experiences.
> Talk, talk, talk when these situations occur.

Have extreme reactions to certain situations, such as hearing a special song, passing certain locations, viewing photographs, and any other reminders of your loved one's death.

> These reactions remind you that you have loved deeply.
> Know that eventually, you will be grateful for the memories.

Fluctuate between accepting the fact of the suicide and not believing it.

> You do know it has happened.
> The full realization seeps in one cell at a time.

Experience some unresolved issues, feelings and conflicts from the past.

Focus on the "if onlys"– been kinder, loved more, listened better.

> You did the best you could.
> You are only human.

You may:

Feel an aching, unrelenting sadness.

Experience difficulty with being alone and being with friends.
      Understand your trust of others is very fragile.
      Trusting will return slowly, but it will return.

Feel as though you no longer fit in anywhere.
      Your new state is uncomfortable.
      It takes time to grow accustomed to this new place.

Struggle with your identity and feelings of insecurity.

Find there are times when all you can do is cry.

Feel trapped in volatile feelings and emotions.
      These will lessen.
      You will not always be so acutely sensitive.

There will be times when you will reel with emotions so powerful that you may question your ability to survive. At other times, you may experience an emotional deadness, as if all feelings are walled away from you. You feel as if something has died on the inside, that a part of you has died, too. Emotions and feelings are survivable, no matter how intense they become. Despite feeling as if you are going crazy, everything you experience during this time is appropriate and normal in this abnormal situation. Fall headlong into your grief. In doing so fully, you will move through it, clearing a path for the future.

Be gentle with yourself, for you are very raw with pain.
You are not responsible for their choice.
You can survive.

There came a time when I decided I would live. Having decided that, I didn't have a clue as to how to go about it. What I recognized one day was that I wanted to do more than just survive my husband's suicide. I wanted substance and meaning in my life.

Moving On: What Helps

Nearly every behavior you have experienced, every feeling that has surfaced, every emotion that has rolled over and through you, every reaction you have had, has been an attempt to adapt to what has happened in your life. Disentangling from an old life is frightening. When a loved one dies, you are challenged to either give up or grow beyond the event. You can be devastated, or you can use the experience, not unlike the magician who transformed metal into gold. You can use this as a marker for personal transformation.

Much in your life can change after a suicide: perspectives and attitudes on life, relationships, beliefs, values, your way of living.

Sometimes people are compelled to travel in totally new directions. Some may grow bitter and withdraw. Some people begin to search for a larger meaning in the deep grief they have experienced.

Adjusting to the world without your loved one takes enormous patience and sensitivity. Your soul is wounded. You are in a process with ups and downs and curves and hills and mountains. It doesn't go straight. It is filled with the light of day and the darkest of nights.

There is a gift in the ashes of despair. Discover the gift.
Use it, and transform your life.

You may:

Experience a significant change in your social support.
>Some people do not know how to express themselves.
>They retreat and remain silent.
>You will need to teach them what you need.

Find yourself searching for a meaning out of the death.

Find that you will always wish you could have prevented the death.
>Remember your humanness.
>Remember that in the best of relationships, there is conflict.

You will need:

To decide to recover and be willing to recover.

To examine old beliefs to see if they fit.

To be willing to discard old beliefs for new ones.

To believe that healing and recovery is possible.

To love yourself enough to be gentle and kind to yourself.

To accept your fearfulness about the unknown.

To be willing to take risks anyway, especially those that move you toward recovery.
>It may mean going to a social gathering for the first time.
>It may mean fixing a leaky faucet.

To learn relaxation techniques or to use what you already know.
>Take walks.
>Feed the birds.
>Meditate.

Your body and spirit are sore, and these are helpful balms. Trust yourself by making an unconditional commitment to yourself. Give yourself permission to take time outs from your grief.

Suddenly, you will find you have gone through nearly a day without being surrounded by crushing pain.

You will need:

To know this is survivable and that you can survive.

To own your pain – acknowledge it – move through it.
Think of pain as a restart button.
Pain serves to remind you that you have lived and loved.
It also reminds you of your discomfort with change.

To redefine who you are without your loved one.

To ask for help.
Seek out those who will listen to you unconditionally.

To enter fully into the event that has come into your life.
Feel it.
Talk about it, talk about it, talk about it.

To shift the focus from your loved one to yourself.
Who am I? What am I about?

You will need:

To redefine your values.

If necessary, to continue asking why.
You will find that you will return to the same answer –
I don't know. I will never know.

To acknowledge your resiliency.
You have managed other crises.
Remember what happened during those times.

To remind yourself of your blessings.
Are you healthy?
Do you have a loving family? Do you have a pet?

To look at regrets you may have and learn from them.
> They teach us to be different in the future.

To explore the question: why did this happen to me?
> It was not done to you.
> It was a choice made by another which profoundly affects you.

To understand that it is a choice to live.

And you will need good people. People with whom you are comfortable, where you can say whatever you want to say, do whatever you feel is necessary for your healing and they will love and support you unconditionally.

It will help to:

Own your aloneness.

Understand that you will re-experience the death of your loved one every time you see a pair of favorite shoes or hear a favorite song.
> You have loved.
> You have memories.
> Move beyond the "if onlys" and "shoulds."
> Focus on short-term goals.
> Allow for periodic surges of grief.
> Redefine your place in your new world.
> Review your relationship with your loved one.
> Take one day at a time.

Know that you will never really know why, that you will probably never understand.

Suicide provokes a journey that can seem endless. It is a journey that can lead you to live more authentically. It means honoring your feelings, whatever they may be at any given moment. It means giving yourself permission to laugh again and to love. And it means patience.

Rebuilding occurs in the quiet hesitant steps taken one at a time. There will be times you falter – you are weary or your wound has been re-opened, and you again experience a flood of hurt and pain. Those moments, however painful, are reminders of your love and involvement with another person. What you do have are memories – snapshots of the sweet and painful times with one no longer present.

Adjusting to the world without your loved one takes time. You have a new role to practice. You will get acquainted with it bit by bit. It may mean adjusting to being single, or parenting one child instead of two. If you lost a parent, it means you have assumed the role of an elder in your family.

Slowly, you will get accustomed to the fact that your loved one is no longer physically present. Your actions and behaviors will reflect that reality as you move forward. The pain will continue to diminish. As you continue to heal, you will be able to talk about your loved one without being overwhelmed by powerful emotions.

There is a gift in the ashes of despair.
Discover the gift. Use it, and transform your life.
This is survivable.

This book is not designed to take the place of therapy. Get professional help at once should you:

> Seriously consider death by suicide.
> Feel life is not worth living.
> Use drugs or alcohol to blot out the pain.
> Be isolated with a sparse support network.

Remember: You will be profoundly changed by this event. You can survive this. This is survivable.

I Remember, I Remember

By Joy Johnson, Centering Resources

In the spring,
when the first crocus pokes its head out of the frozen ground
I think of you and I remember. . .
I remember. . .
In the summer,
when the blaring heat wilts the rose petals
and paints unsightly cracks in the ground,
I think of you and I remember. . .
I remember. . .
In the autumn,
when the trees are ablaze in the glory of fall
and my shoes make crackling sounds as I walk,
I think of you and I remember. . .
I remember.
And in the winter, when I stand at my window
to watch a blizzard whirl snow
around my grief and loneliness
then, too, I think of you and I remember. . .
I remember.

About the Author

Sondra Sexton-Jones was born in Dallas, Texas. Ms. Sexton-Jones has lived in Alaska since 1993, currently residing in Juneau. Ms. Sexton-Jones is a Licensed Professional Counselor, Certified Thanatologist, and traumatologist, and maintains a private practice. She frequently works with survivors of suicide, individuals having endured losses by violent means, and first responders. She is currently pursuing a doctorate in trauma and crisis. She divides her time between Alaska and Texas.

Her family has grown since the death of her husband, Ray, to six grown grandchildren and three great grandchildren. Ray has missed birthdays, weddings and births. At all the events, silently, we think of our two family members who are missing: Ray, by his suicide, and daughter, Deirdre, killed in 2013 by an impaired driver as she drove to work.

These losses have taught Sondra that life does go on, and we can fashion our lives to include happiness going forward without leaving the memories behind of our loved ones. Sondra Sexton-Jones specialize in offering grief therapy resulting from violent deaths.

For more information about Sondra visit:
https://www.sondrasextonjones.com